I AM PHENOMENAL

A Collection of Affirmation Quotes

Written by:
Mrs. Sherneice Gatewood-Alli and
Ms. Quanasha Gatewood

Copyright © 2021 by Sherneice and Quanasha Gatewood.

ISBN: 978-0-578-88088-4

All rights reserved. No part of this book may be reproduced or transmitted in any form or by any means, electronic or mechanical, including photocopying, recording, or by any information storage and retrieval system, without permission in writing from the copyright owner.

This book was printed in the United States of America.

About Us

My name is Quanasha Gatewood and I am a 28-year-old survivor of domestic violence and abuse.

I am a partner and author of this journal book with my sister.

Writing this journal book with my sister was a way to heal from some harsh words I've heard in my life and actually turn it into quotes.

For me, physical abuse was the easier form of DV to heal from. Rewiring my brain to believe I am phenomenal is an ongoing process.

I said the most powerful words I never ever thought I would have said, "I am a domestic violence survivor."

I was not completely free and since I said those words I have unlocked A Whole New World for myself and I learned I am not alone. I have met a whole community of survivors and they showed me that I have the strength to get through and also showed me that I have the strength to get someone else through. I hope this book helps women of all ages find peace within themselves so that their self-love Journey can start today.

My name is Sherneice Gatewood-Alli and I have been a survivor of domestic violence for 20+ years. I decided I would no longer be someone's punching bag or allow someone to verbally abuse me. I thought the person loved me. So finally, 7 years later I found a safe way out of the relationship.

I am now a certified Domestic Violence Life Coach and CEO of an not-for-profit organization, We Are Phenomenal Women Inc., educating others on what is domestic violence and the different types of abuse.

I asked my sister to be a part of this book because I know this will bring us closer due to her and I having experienced the same types of abuse.

I hope our quotes, assignments and the beautiful pictures will help your self care process.

Thank you for your support.

Dedication

I would like to take the time out to dedicate this book to everyone who may be suffering in silence. I would like to say you are not alone. Inside are some beautiful pictures, empowering quotes and some self-reflective assignments.

> Remember this book is for you my sister who never said "**I AM A SURVIVOR**" out loud.

From *Sherneice* and *Quanasha Gatewood*

We would like to say thank you for purchasing this book, however from Queens to Queens we would like to know how do you feel? Choose one and write about your feelings on the opposite page.

I feel frustrated.

I feel grateful.

I feel happy.

I feel honored/blessed.

I feel hurt.

I feel love.

I am not sure how I feel.

I feel stressed

I feel alone.

I am a Phenomenal Woman and I demand my power now.
I am powerful woman.
I am wise and gorgeous.
I am deserving of love and respect.
I am my own woman.
I am a Queen!

- Sherneice Gatewood-Alli

From every wound there is a scar, and every scar tells a story A story that says I survived

– Fr.Craig Scott

Write down five things that make you proud to say I AM a Survivor!

1. _____

2. _____

3. _____

4. _____

5. _____

Express Your Thoughts Queen

The weak can
Never forgive,
Forgiveness
Is the attribute of the
STRONG

-Mahatma Gandhi

Name three times when you did not want to forgive, but then you realized you must Forgive in order to be Strong.

1. ....

2. ....

3. ....

What do you see? Do you see your reflection as a POWERFUL & STRONG WOMAN ?

The MOST
revengeful thing you can do
is REGAIN your PEACE.

- Quanasha Gatewood

Steps on how to Regain your Peace

1. Realize and Recognize someone or something is destroying your PEACE.

   ....

   ....

   ....

2. What brings me serenity?

   ....

   ....

   ....

3. Are you willing to LET IT GO

   ....

   ....

   ....

4. Are you ready to do some Spring Cleaning.

   ....

   ....

   ....

Here are some examples Of Regaining your peace

- Carry your peace with you.

- Think peaceful thoughts.

- Pause between thoughts to create space in your mind.

- Close windows in your brain when it becomes cluttered. So you can return back to peace.

- Explore different types meditation.

- Practice what works for you regardless of what works for others.

- I am at peace with my meditation practice.

- Seek peace within. When you create inner peace, your outer world becomes more peaceful

Name some ways you can let somebody or something GO!

We must develop and maintain the capacity to forgive. He who is devoid of the power to forgive is devoid of the power to LOVE

- Martin Luther King

What do you need in order to love again?

Never forget that walking away from something unhealthy is brave even if you stumble a little on your way out the door

- unknown

Name three times when you did not want to forgive, but then you realized you must Forgive in order to be Strong.

1. ....

2. ....

3. ....

4. ....

5. ....

Trauma creates change you don't choose. Healing is about creating change you do choose.

- Michelle Rosenthall

Don't let someone who doesn't know your value tell you how much you're worth

- unknown

Say to yourself three times everyday
I AM WORTHY of

....

....

....

....

....

....

....

....

....

....

I decided to give myself a
GIFT
A GIFT to love all of me
Love my thoughts
Love my ambition
Love my space
Love peace
Love my brilliance
Love my soul
And no one can take this
GIFT

- Quanasha Gatewood

When was the last time you gave yourself a GIFT and what was it?

1. ....

2. ....

3. ....

4. ....

5. ....

Learned behaviors can be unlearned as long as you recognize that behavior you was taught isn't your FAULT

— Sherneice Gatewood-Alli

What behaviors were you taught but you realize this is not the right way?

You can't start
The next
Chapter of your life if you
keep
Rereading the
Last ONE

- Unknown

Name a time in your life when your past is hindering your present?

How did you overcome this?

A wise women
Wishes to be no one's enemy
a wise women
refuses to be
Anyone victim

- Maya Angelou

At any given moment you have the power to say this is not how the story is going to end.

- Christine Mason Miller

Reflection

Name a couple of conflicts you had with others and write down three ways you could resolve the issue.

1. ....
....
....

2. ....
....
....

3. ....
....
....

This is a part of the book where We would like for you to do some soul searching of self by answering some questions and writing down your notes.

Learn the true you, learn who you are as a Queen!,

What do you like to do for yourself.

Where do you like to go?

Where is your happy place)

When was the last time you made yourself happy?

What had prevented you from achieving your Goals?

What are your Biggest challenges?

What would you like MORE of in your life? Who INSPIRES you? WHO Drains you?

What do you SECRETLY need to acknowledge in your life?

Tips on how to love thyself

1. Everyday for a couple of hours

    Turn off the TV and unplug from social media for 15 minutes to get centered while self- pampering. Light a candle and listen to soothing music and give time to oneself to understand how Blessed you are.

2. Understand your body is a loving vessel

    Treating your body like a loving vessel will not only boost your self-love but also your energy. Be intentional about what you put into your body, not only because you want to look good but because you want to feel good. Feeding your body nutrient rich food will have you oozing love out of your pores.

3. Explore your spirituality

Faith is the foundation for self-love, no matter what you believe. Believing in something opens up your soul to the beauty of belief and trust. It will build your intuition and help you make decisions based on your gut. When your explore your spirituality it will also take you on a journey to learning things about yourself and those new thoughts, feelings, passions, and raw emotions will make you appreciate yourself even more.

4. Find your happy place

Think of a place that makes it simple to just be. That means being able to sit quietly and embrace the here and now, not thinking about what's due at work or what bills need to be paid. You owe this happy place to yourself. Self- love is all about connecting with yourself, and one of the easiest places to do that is to make yourself happy.

We are proud to say you made it to the end of journal book. Now from Queens to Queens, we would like to know how do you feel now? Choose one and write about your feelings on the opposite page.

I feel frustrated.

I feel grateful.

I feel happy.

I feel honored/blessed.

I feel hurt.

I feel love.

I am not sure how I feel.

I feel stressed

I feel alone.

What was your favorite assignment
Journal Notes

What was your favorite assignment
Journal Notes

What was your favorite assignment
Journal Notes

What was your favorite assignment
Journal Notes

www.ingramcontent.com/pod-product-compliance
Lightning Source LLC
Chambersburg PA
CBHW042003150426
43194CB00002B/108